YOUR KNOWLEDGE HAS VALUE

- We will publish your bachelor's and master's thesis, essays and papers

- Your own eBook and book - sold worldwide in all relevant shops

- Earn money with each sale

Upload your text at www.GRIN.com and publish for free

Harry Altmann

Kingship in Anglo-Saxon England. A Comparison of Oswald and Edmund as Royal Saints

Bibliographic information published by the German National Library:

The German National Library lists this publication in the National Bibliography; detailed bibliographic data are available on the Internet at http://dnb.dnb.de .

This book is copyright material and must not be copied, reproduced, transferred, distributed, leased, licensed or publicly performed or used in any way except as specifically permitted in writing by the publishers, as allowed under the terms and conditions under which it was purchased or as strictly permitted by applicable copyright law. Any unauthorized distribution or use of this text may be a direct infringement of the author s and publisher s rights and those responsible may be liable in law accordingly.

Imprint:

Copyright © 2013 GRIN Verlag GmbH
Print and binding: Books on Demand GmbH, Norderstedt Germany
ISBN: 978-3-656-92803-4

This book at GRIN:

http://www.grin.com/en/e-book/295096/kingship-in-anglo-saxon-england-a-comparison-of-oswald-and-edmund-as-royal

GRIN - Your knowledge has value

Since its foundation in 1998, GRIN has specialized in publishing academic texts by students, college teachers and other academics as e-book and printed book. The website www.grin.com is an ideal platform for presenting term papers, final papers, scientific essays, dissertations and specialist books.

Visit us on the internet:

http://www.grin.com/

http://www.facebook.com/grincom

http://www.twitter.com/grin_com

English Department
Summer Term 2013
Seminar: Two Anglo-Saxon Kings and Their Lives
Harry Altmann
Date: 23.07.2013

Kingship in Anglo-Saxon England
A Comparison of Oswald and Edmund as Royal Saints

2. Sem. 2-Fach-MA. English, Sport

Table of Contents

1. Introduction 3
2. Kingship in Anglo-Saxon England.. 3
3. The Author: Ælfric of Eynsham 6
4. The Genre 6
   4.1 The Importance of Saints 6
   4.2 Saints' Lives – a Typical Christian Genre... 8
   4.3 Oswald of Northumbria 8
   4.4 Edmund the Martyr 9
   4.5 A Comparison of *vita* and *passio* 9
5. Linguistic Analysis.. 10
   5.1 The Sources 10
   5.2 Overall Structures of the Texts.. 11
   5.3 Syntactic Structure 13
   5.4 Style and Alliterative Elements... 14
   5.5 Comparison of the Description of the Murders Oswald and Edmund 15
6. Conclusion... 17
7. References 18
8. Appendix 19

1. Introduction

The basic form of society in Anglo-Saxon England was a kingdom. Over the centuries the movement was away from many small units to larger kingdoms controlling greater populations. The first kings were pagan and when Christianity became established the Christian kings kept many of the characteristics of their pagan forebears. The Christian kings continued to be primarily military leaders.

A cult of martyrs arose in Anglo-Saxon England which included Christian kings who had died either in battle or in defence of Christianity. Other royal saints followed a different path to sainthood by leading exemplary Christian lives.

Many saints' lives composed in Latin circulated in Anglo-Saxon England but it was the monk and author Ælfric of Eynsham who translated a collection of saints' lives into Old English. In particular this paper will deal with the lives of St Edmund and St Oswald. After a brief introduction to the lives of these two saints an analysis of the two concepts of *vita* and *passio* follows. Then the general and syntactic linguistic structure of both texts is examined. Finally a comparison of the deaths of St Oswald and St Edmund illustrates the difference in approach of these writings.

2. Kingship in Anglo-Saxon England

Kingship in Anglo-Saxon England seems to have been widespread by the end of the sixth century. Myths survive which depict the founders of some of the kingdoms as defeating British rulers in battle in the late fifth and sixth centuries. By the eighth century Anglo-Saxon rulers showed a desire to connect with the Germanic heroes of the early fourth and fifth centuries, but this is unlikely to be solid fact (Lapidge 1999: 271). Unfortunately not many written sources are available for the "Lost Centuries" from 400 to 600. Therefore not much is known about the establishment of kingdoms at that time. So according to Yorke: "[n]ot only are the birth pangs of kingship among the Anglo-Saxons lost to us, but it is also difficult to say exactly what the position of king meant to an early Anglo-Saxon." (Yorke 2003).

Anglo-Saxon kings used their claimed descent from pagan gods to back up their power through divine authority and to establish their family as the only legitimate lineage for future kings. Two strands of kingships can be made out: rulership exercising political and religious functions and military leadership. The position of kings at this time was based ultimately on their ability as war leaders and accounts of these kings relate their victories in battle over British kings. Entries in the Anglo-Saxon Chronicle give insight into aggressiveness of the kingdoms in relation both to territorial competitiveness and collection of tribute and booty (Yorke 2003).

Within the society the loyalty between a lord and his retainers was crucial and this basic principle did not change with Christianization. A clear impression of how a royal court at that time functioned is given by the poem *Beowulf.*

> A king lives surrounded by noble warriors, who feast with him, sleep in his hall by night, fight for him and are ready, or anyway hoped to be ready, to die for him. Their number and royalty are crucial to royal power (Campbell 1982: 54)

The poem stresses how the relationship between king and warband was reciprocal. The king provided upkeep for his warriors and rewarded them with gifts and in return the followers fought loyally in battle (Yorke 2003: 17). Despite pressure from their followers to be granted land, kings managed to preserve the principle that they kept inalienable rights over land which encompassed the right to military service (Lapidge 1999: 271).

Kingdoms at this time were continuously trying to enlarge their area of control. They have been referred to as a heptarchy consisting of Northumbria, Mercia, East Anglia, Essex, Kent, Sussex and Wessex but this is an oversimplification. "For example, we hear of kings of Wight, of the West Midland kingdoms of the *Hwicce* and the *Magonsaete*, and of Lindsey. There were probably others of whom we know nothing" (Campbell 1982: 53). Due to intermarriage and competition kingdoms amalgamated leading to only four Anglo-Saxon kingdoms remaining at the beginning of the ninth century: East Anglia, Mercia, Northumbria and Wessex (Lapidge 1999: 271). In addition, by the end of the sixth century the most powerful kings had consolidated their power to the point where they were able to claim overlordship over the rest, their power extending over most of the Anglo-Saxon lands. The Anglo-Saxon Chronicle calls these kings *bretwaldas* or rulers over Britain (Campbell 1982: 53).

Archaeological evidence shows that the most important concern for the leaders of the early pagan kingdoms was war, shown by the burial at Sutton Hoo of not only everyday weapons but ceremonial war gear (Yorke 2003: 16). By 600 royal authority had extended from his immediate followers to other subjects of his kingdom. The earliest surviving lawcode is that of Æthelbert of Kent and shows the king as responsible for the maintenance of law and order. This legislation covered all ranks of society from nobles to slaves. The king set and enforced the payments which a transgressor was liable to pay to the victim of his action. This system was important to prevent an accident resulting in a bloodfeud. This aspect of law enforcement was of benefit to the king as he received a percentage of fines (Yorke 2003: 18).

The authority of the earliest Anglo-Saxon kings was based on Germanic traditions but there were other influences from the contemporary Germanic world, most importantly from Francia. Especially in Kent, food, drink and dress of the nobility were modelled on Frankish taste (Yorke 2033: 18).

Bede in his *Ecclesiastical History* gives little sense of how Anglo-Saxon England built on its Romano-British background. Only recently has it come to be appreciated that Anglo-Saxon kingdoms were organized on the basis of Roman and sub-Roman principles (Yorke 2003: 19).

> There is good reason to suppose that here [Bernicia], and in other areas of the north the system of local organization and government was one not so much created by the Anglo-Saxons as taken over by them from the Britons (Campbell 1982: 58).

Most of the inhabitants of Anglo-Saxon England were of Romano-British origin and the Anglo-Saxon kings used the trappings of the Roman past. Bede writes in his *Ecclesiastical History of the English People* how Edwin of Northumbria was preceded by banners and the type of standard which the Romans call a *tufa* and the English call a *thuf*.

The adoption of Christianity by all the Anglo-Saxon royal houses during the seventh century helped the development of kingship. Kings found Christianity attractive because of the role it gave them as Christ's representative. Kings were the most important benefactors of the religious houses within their kingdoms. Christianity brought new concepts such as Roman land law, literacy and classical learning to the Anglo-Saxons (Lapidge 1999: 271).

3. The Author: Ælfric of Eynsham

In the medieval period the perception of authorship differed considerably from today's view. The idea of an author as an independent artist is a product of the Renaissance. In contrast to most manuscripts of the Middle Ages, the authorship of the *Life of Saints* is known.

Ælfric of Eynsham was born in c. 955 and died in c. 1010. Not much is known about his family background. He received his education in the monastic school of Winchester under Bishop Æthelwold. After becoming a monk and priest he was sent as a teacher in around 987 to the newly founded abbey of Cerne Abbas. Most of the works that have come down to us are believed to have been composed there. In 1005 he became the first abbot of the refounded abbey Eynsham, where he also died some five years later (Lapidge 1999: 8).

He was one of the most learned scholars of his time, and was widely read in his own time. Today, he is best known for his prose works written in the Old English vernacular, the most important of which are the *Sermones Catholici*, two series of 40 homilies on the Gospels, *Lives of Saints, Excerptions de Are Grammatica* (a grammar of Latin), a translation of Genesis into Old English, and some letters (Lapidge 1999: 8).

His elegantly-written vernacular prose works were widely read in his own time. "Ælfric was, within his limitations, a formidable and important writer. He is the father, the inventor, of the rich tradition of plainly stated, undecorated, but vigorous and powerful English prose" (Campbell 1982: 203).

4. The Genre

4.1 The Importance of Saints

Almost since the establishment of the Christian church saints have been venerated. To become a saint a man or woman must stand out on account of outstanding moral conduct. This often occurred in connection with religious persecution and a violent death. On Christianity becoming the official state religion of the Roman empire in the fourth century, a new aspect of the veneration of saints emerged. Not only was the saint commemorated, but veneration of their relics became common. Ælfric describes the reliquary cult at St Lawrence's tomb in Rome in the *Life of St Edmund* (II. 303-8).

The cult of saints and their relics spread as Christianity conquered Europe in the sixth and seventh centuries. The saints role was as mediator between people and God.

> The focus of people's attention in an Anglo-Saxon church, therefore, was the shrine of the saint who could intercede with God on behalf of the petitioning sufferer or sinner. We should not imagine that the saints were conceived abstractly as disembodied spirits. Theirs was a physical and palpable presence; that is to say, that saint was physically present in each shrine insofar as that shrine contained a relic of his/ her body – a bone, a fingernail, a lock of hair, whatever. A contact with the saint's miraculous power could be established by touching that relic (Lapidge 1999: 243).

The relic did not even have to be a physical part of the saint as an object which he had touched was also able to pass on the miraculous power.

In Anglo-Saxon times the Holy See had not yet taken control of the canonization of saints. The efficacy of the saint's relics was the essential criterion for canonization. The local church was able to recognize a new saint solely on the basis of having lived a holy life and after death having accomplished miraculous cures through his relics. Especially in the late Anglo-Saxon period there was intense competition between churches as to the importance of the saints whose relics they possessed. This encouraged the creation of new saints (Lapidge 1999: 245).

The established view of the cults of murdered and martyred royal saints of Anglo-Saxon is that they are of political origin. It was a matter of prestige for royal houses to be able to point to a saint among their ancestors. However, the view is also held that their cults originated in lay devotion to innocent victims and that many elements of paganism were incorporated in the beliefs and practices that accompanied them.

> Thacker argues that Oswald's cult was at first neglected by the church, originated among the laity and was taken up by his royal kin before ecclesiastical interest began, and that it betrays a number of characteristics of pagan or pre-Christian beliefs (Cubitt 2003: 61-2).

It has been suggested that the Anglo-Saxon tradition of the veneration of murdered royal saints is unparalleled elsewhere in the same period, even when looking at areas which influenced the early English church (Rollason 1982: 14).

4.2 Saints' Lives – a Typical Christian Genre

With the increasing veneration of saints came the need to gather information and produce written reports of their lives. The prototype for saints' lives was Sulpicius Severus' *Life of St Martin*. He was a Roman author who lived in the late fourth and early fifth century in Gaul. Venantius Fortunatus was another famous author of saints' lives, living 150 years later as a contemporary of Pope Gregory the Great. Despite his classical literary education he chose to use a simple and straightforward style in writing his saints' lives. He wrote the *Life of Radegung*, the Merowingian queen whose friend he was, and who was later canonized. This life became the archetype of medieval lives of saints who where of noble or royal descent and had lived an ideal Christian life.

4.3 Oswald of Northumbria

Oswald (c. 604 – 642) was King of Northumbria from 634 until his death in 642. During the reign of King Edwin he was exiled among the Scots of Dal Riada where he was converted to Christianity. After defeating Cadwallon if Gwynedd in battle at Heavenfield he was acknowledged as king in both Bernicia and Deira. It is difficult to determine the extent of his authority; Bede's claim that he was overlord over the British, Pictish, Irish and English people is probably inflated but for most of his reign he was overlord of all the English kingdoms south of the Humber. The fact that all was quiet between 633 and 641 is evidence of the effectiveness of his overlordship. His strategy in overlordship and alliances was aimed at containing the growing power of Penda of Mercia (Lapidge 1999: 347). It appears that it was only Penda's resistance which stood in the way of the establishment of a loosely compacted kingdom under Northumbrian rule (Stenton 1971: 81-2).

Soon after becoming king Oswald asked the monastery of Iona for help to convert Northumbria to Christianity. He was sent Bishop Aidan to whom he gave as his see the island of Lindisfarne, close to the principal Bernician stronghold of Bamburgh. Bede described

Oswald as 'the most Christian king', who was personally involved in the development of the church in Northumbria (Lapidge 1999: 347).

Oswald was killed by Penda of Mercia in 642 at the battle of *Maserfeld*. "Nothing is recorded of the events which lead up to the battle, nor of his incidents beyond the tradition that Oswald was hear to pray for the souls of his army as his enemies closed in on hin" (Stenton 1971: 82). Immediately after there were reports of miracles at the place of his death. "His cult was established at the monastery of Bardney of Lincolnshire where he became venerated as the first Anglo-Saxon royal saint, whose popularity reached continental Europe" (Lapidge 1999: 348).

4.4 Edmund the Martyr

Almost nothing is known of Edmund the Martyr (Old English: *Eadmund*, *ēad*, "prosperity", "riches"; and *mund*, "protector"). His death is noted in the *Anglo-Saxon Chronicle* at the hands of a Viking army in 869. No evidence of his reign apart from a number of coins remains. After his death he was venerated as a saint.

The first written account of Edmund's death was produced by Abbo of Fleury who taught in England in Ramsey from 985 to 987. There are grounds for assuming that Abbo's account of Edmund's martyrdom after the battle could be true, although this contradicts the *Anglo-Saxon Chronicle's* statement that he died in battle. It could be that the *Chronicle* telescoped the events together. "[T]he early development of his cult suggests very strongly that a basis of fact underlay the legend of his martyrdom" (Stenton 1971: 248). Discoveries of coins dated c. 903 show that the recognition of Edmund as a saint is likely to have started within a quarter of a century of his death.

4.5 A Comparison of *vita* and *passio*

By the early Middle Ages two basic concepts of saints' lives had evolved, the *passio* ("passion") and the *vita* ("life").

The *passio* was the literary form appropriate for a saint who had been martyred for his/her faith, whereas the *vita* properly pertained to a confessor (that is, a saint who's impeccable service to God constituted an metaphorical, not real, martyrdom) (Lapidge 1999: 252).

The classic *passio* is an account of how a saint of noble birth adopts Christianity in a pagan society. This saint is brought before the authorities and told to recant by sacrificing to the pagan gods which he refuses to do, even when tortured excruciatingly. These tortures are described in gruesome detail. The saint is then executed, normally by beheading.

In contrast a *vita* takes the following form. The nobly-born saint's birth is accompanied by miraculous portents, he excels at learning and then turns from secular to holy life, which means giving up his family. He makes his way through the various stages of the church and performs miracles while still alive. On seeing his approaching death he dies peacefully after giving instruction to his followers. After his death miracles occur at his tomb (Lapidge 1999: 251).

Of course, it is also possible for a saint's life to combine elements of both *vita* and *passio*, where the course of the saint's life is shown to be exemplary but is ended by martyrdom. This is the case in Ælfric's *Life of Oswald*, whereas Edmund's life conforms to the classic concept of the *passio*.

5. Linguistic Analysis

5.1 The Sources

Most of the lives of saints which were composed by Ælfric in Old English are based on Latin originals. Since the seventeenth century saints' lives in Latin had been widely read in Anglo-Saxon England but it was Ælfric who was the first to translate a significant number into the vernacular. His collection of forty lives followed up on the two series of Catholic Homilies which he had already written. The edited version of the *St Oswald, King and Martyr* used here is from volume two of Ælfric's *Lives of Saints*, edited and revised by Walter Skeat and published by the *Early English Text Society*, Oxford 1900, pages 125-143. The text *The Passion of St Edmund, King and Martyr* is gratefully taken from Mitchell and Robinson 1992, pages 195-203.

The original text of *The Life of St Oswald* was composed by Bede in his *Historia Ecclesiastica*. He was one of the most outstanding personalities of the Anglo-Saxon period. Bede was sent to the twin monastery of Monkwearmouth and Jarrow as a young boy and spent almost all his life there. He received a classical education and wrote almost only in Latin. Bede wrote commentaries on the Old and New Testament as well as works on science and chronology, educational works and poems.

He is most famous for his five volumes of the *Historia Ecclesiastica Gentis Anglorum*, or *An Ecclesiastical History of the English People*. Not only does this work supply most of what we know today about pre-conquest English history, but it also supplied the basis the basis of the *Anglo-Saxon Chronicle*, ordered by King Alfred 150 years later.

> In the first place, Bede's life and work constitute the most important monument, and the most striking symbol, of the highly dramatic cultural changes that followed the conversion of the Anglo-Saxons (Campbell 1982: 70).

The original text of *The Passion of St Edmund, King and Martyr* was by the learned monk Abbo of Fleury. Abbo's text shows how the story of Edmund had been developed in both monastic and popular traditions, including Abbo's own treatment of Edmund as the ideal Christian king. Ælfric's text was not a straight forward translation, which may be explained by a difference in purpose as Ælfric wanted to write a sermon to move and instruct the common people while Abbo had written an elaborate hagiographical text.

5.2 Overall Structures of the Texts

The Catholic Homilies were definitely written to be used as sermons in church, but it is not clear whether the *Lives of the Saints* were intended for the same purpose, or were rather intended as devotional reading. However during this period all reading was either out loud or the reader moved his lips so they are definitely intended to be presented orally (Needham 1976: 23).

The structure of Ælfric's account of Edmund is characteristic of a saint's life, in particular the genre of the *passio*. He first gives a source for the narrative (ll. 126-36), then describes the exemplary qualities that Edmund manifested (ll. 137-46). A long middle section (ll. 147-222) details his martyrdom. The longest section of the work describes what happened to his body after his beheading and the miracles which happened before and after his burial.

Looking at the structure of Ælfric's account of Oswald, a different structure can be ascertained. This narrative structure is suited to a *vita*. The narrative consists of many short units which taken together tell the complete story of Oswald's life from his youth to his death and beyond that to the many miracles which occur and convince even doubters of his sainthood. There is no real introduction, but the narrative starts immediately with Oswald's youth and victory against Cadwalla (ll. 1-28). Then follows an account of miracles through the cross (ll. 30-44). From line 44 to line 86 Oswald's invitation to Aiden is described. After that the blessing of Oswald's right hand is described (ll. 87-103). Lines 104 to 117 describe the growth of his lordship and his devotion. From line 118 to 144 the story of the holy Berinius is told. From line 144 the narrative takes a turn with the threat of war from Penda and the death of Oswald in battle. The next passage deals with what happened to his body and the many and diverse miracles which occurred in connection his relics or secondary relics (ll. 169-271). The conclusion sums up the saintliness of Oswald (ll. 272-288).

Ælfric, basing his narrative on Bede's account, is relating Oswald's biography, based on historical facts which at least in part have been verified. The focus is not on his martyrdom but on his life and the miracles which occurred before and after his death. The events are rather loosely strung together and the tone is often conversational. For example both lines 45 and 60 start with *Hwæt* which can be translated as "Well then!" or "Lo then!", although a modern English story teller might say "well" or "anyway".

At the end of both texts the lord is invoked and the final word in each text is 'Amen'.

5.3 Syntactic Structure

Old English has an inflectional system which includes strong and weak forms of adjectives and distinguishes only the simple present and past tenses, and employs a third element (or word), order Subject ... Verb as well as the familiar Subject Verb and Verb Subject (Lapidge 1999: 438).

However, Old English is on the way to Modern English, with inflectional endings being lost and a tendency to rely on the order Subject Verb Object to distinguish subject from object (Lapidge 1999: 438).

Old English prose has a basically paratactic structure as opposed to Modern English's hypotactic style. Parataxis is defined as "[a] syntactic construction in which clauses or phrases are linked without the use of subordinating conjunctions [...]" (Hogg 1992: 544). Hypotaxis is "[a] term in syntax which refers to the sequencing of constituents by means of subordinating conjunctions [...]" (Hogg 1992: 542).

In Old English prose texts an indicator of the paratactic style is a series of independent main clauses or sentences all starting with the adverb **þā**. One might consider this to be an unsophisticated style, comparable to how children relate a story, but **þā** translates not only as the adverb 'then' but also as the subordinator 'when'.

The following extract from *St Edmund* (ll. 251-55) illustrates this point:

Eft þa on fyrste, æfter fela gearum,
þa seo hergung geswac
and sibb wearð forgifen þam geswenctan folce,
þa fengon hi togædere
and worhton ane cyrcan wurðlice þam halgan,
forþanðe gelome wundra wurdon æt his byrgene,
æt þam gebædhuse þær he bebyrged wæs.

Then, after many years, when harrying had ceased and peace was restored to the oppressed people, they came together and built a church worthily in honour of the saint, because miracles had frequently been done at its burial place, even at the chapel where he was buried.

It can be seen how, when the prose is set out in the line form of verse, all instances of þā appear at the beginning of the line. It is clear that the first instance of þā means 'then' while the second can best be translated as 'when' while the third instance could also translated as 'then' but may be left out altogether. This example shows that a complex sentence structure may be achieved despite the repeated use of þā. Two main clauses linked by 'and' are embedded within two dependent clauses, one a temporal and one a causal clause.

In contrast the following extract from *St Oswald* illustrates the use of þā to introduce a new event (ll. 162-165):

> Þa het se hæþena cynincg his heafod ofaslean
> and his swiðran earm, and settan hi to myrcelse.
> Þa æfter Oswoldes slege, feng Oswig his broðor
> to Norðhymbra rice [...]

> Then the heathen king commanded the strike of his head
> and his right arm, and to set them up as a mark [trophy].
> Then after the slaying of Oswald his brother Oswy
> succeeded to the kingdom of Northumbria

In both texts on the saints' lives there is frequent use of þā at the beginning of the sentence. These many instances of þā indicate a large number of events which are being brought into an order.

5.4 Style and Alliterative Elements

Just as in contemporary English literature a distinction is made in Old English literature between poetry and prose and it is clear that Ælfric's *Lives of Saints* qualify as prose. However, his prose draws on stylistic elements which are also found in verse. The prose of *Lives of Saints* is rhythmical in a similar to way to the alliterative verse of *Beowulf,* but freer in form.

> The manuscripts of the homilies, like all Old English manuscripts – including those of texts in verse – are written continuously. The homilies, however, are found to consist of

an unbroken series of pairs of short phrases, usually linked together by alliteration; the phrases are all of about equal length, and each as a rule contains two stressed syllables (Needham 1976: 21).

In the following example of St Edmund the alliterative rhyme patterns can be clearly seen when the text is set in long lines with the alliterations underlined:

Eadmund se eadiga	Eastengla cyning
wæssnotor and wurðfull	and wurðode symble
mid æþelum þeawum	þone ælmihtigan God
He wæs eadmod and geþungen,	and swa anræde þurhwunode
Þæt he nolde abugan	to bysmorfullum leahtrum
ne on naþre healfe	he ne ahylde his þeawas,
ac wæs symble gemyndig	þære soþan lare,
þu eart to heafodmen geset,	ne ahefe þu ðe,
ac beo betwux mannum	swa swa an man of him.

(ll. 137-43)

However, Ælfric does not use other stylistic features of Old English verse such as its diction and use of variation, and rhythm and alliteration are not rigidly used (Needham 1976: 22).

He was a conscious stylist, but explicitly rejected the obscure vocabulary and convoluted syntax which was fashionable in contemporary Anglo-Latin writings and even in the vernacular, and created instead an elegant an balanced prose using simpler vocabulary and structures (Lapidge 1999: 9).

5.5 Comparison of the Description of the Murders Oswald and Edmund

As argued above, Oswald's life follows the form of a *vita* and Edmund's of a *passio* which means that the weight given to the actual martyrdom is very different. In the *Life of Oswald* his death is introduced by a factual descriptions of how he was 38 years old at the time of his death. Then Ælfric tells how Penda, king of the Mercians, made war on

Oswald. There is an element of *passio* in that Oswald meets his death as a true Christian commending his soul and the souls of his followers to God. However, there is no lengthy description of torture leading up to the death. The actual death is over in two lines (ll. 162-63).

> Þa geseah he genealecan his lifes geendunge
> and gebæd for his folc þe þær feallende sweolt
> and betæhte heora sawla and hine sylfne Gode
> and þus clypode on his fylle, "God gemiltsa urum sawlum."
>
> (ll. 156-161)

The description of the events leading up to Edmund's death are more vividly described. Perhaps this can be ascribed to the fact that very little is actually known, and was then known, about how Edmund died. So Abbo and following him Ælfric were able to use their imaginations. The language used is more metaphorical. In line 151 Hinguar and Hubba are described as associated by the devil: "geanlæhte þurh deofol". Additionally Hinguar in line 157 is described as being like a wolf: "And se foresæda Hinguar færlice swa swa wulf on lande bestalcode".

It is noticeable that there is more use of direct speech in the *Life of Edmund* which makes it much livelier and more dramatic reading (or listening). There is a series of direct utterances between the messenger, king Edmund and the bishop (ll. 164-196).

In contrast to Oswald's death that of Edmund is described in great detail. Edmund's death is a classic Christian martyrdom. The tortures he must suffer are related in detail over 16 lines (ll. 204-220). Edmund's martyrdom links him with Christ, St Peter and Sebastian.

6. Conclusion

Examining the historical background of kingship in the Anglo-Saxon period it becomes clear how the idea of the king as martyr was an important theme for how the English saw their history.

Both texts of the *Life of St Edmund* and the *Life of St Oswald* can be seen as representing the genre of saints' lives in an ideal way. Edmund's life is the prototype of the concept of *passio*, whereas Oswald's life mainly consists of *vita* incorporating a few elements of *passio*.

Further it becomes clear that Ælfric was not just a translator of Latin texts but one of the most prominent authors of late Anglo-Saxon prose. His 'rhythmical' prose style can be experienced in his *Lives of Saints*. He makes use of stylistic and linguistic elements such as direct speech and alliterative elements to emphasize the drama of his *passio*.

An analysis of the murder of Oswald and Edmund shows how different concepts of saints' lives have been established. Analysing and comparing the overall structure of the texts underlines this difference. Particularly examining the introduction to and the actual death of the saints gives insight into the two concepts of *passio* and *vita*.

7. References

Campbell, James. John, Eric. Wormald, Patrick. 1982. *The Anglo-Saxons.* Penguin Books Ltd, London

Cubitt, Catherine. 2003. *Sites and sanctity: revisiting the cult of murdered and martyred Anglo-Saxon royal saints.* Blackwell Publishers Ltd, Maldon

Hall, J. R. Clark. 1960. *A Concise Anglo-Saxon Dictionary.* Cambridge University Press, Cambridge

Hogg, Richard M. 1992. *The Cambridge History of the English Language. Volume 1. The Beginnings to 1066.* Cambridge University Press, Cambridge

Langenscheidt, Collins. 2004. *Großwörterbuch English.* Langenscheidt Verlag, München

Lapidge, Michael; Blair, John; Keynes, Simon; Scragg, Donald (eds). 1999. *The Blackwell Encyclopedia of Anglo-Saxon England.* Blackwell Publishers Ltd, Maldon

McLaughlin, John. 1983. *Old English Syntax. A Handbook.* Max Niemeyer Verlag, Tübingen

Mitchell, Bruce and Robinson, Fred C.. 1992. *A Guide to Old English.* Blackwell Publishers Ltd, Oxford

Needham, G. I.. 1976. *Ælfric. Lives of Three English Saints.* University of Exeter, Exeter

Rollason, David. 1982. *The Cults of Murdered Royal Saints in Anglo-Saxon England.* Cambridge University Press, Cambridge

Stenton, Frank. 1971. *Anglo-Saxon England.* Oxford University Press, Oxford.

Yorke, Barbera. 2003. *Kings and Kingdoms of Early Anglo-Saxon England.* Routledge, London.

8. Appendix

Plagiierte Hausarbeiten

Ein Plagiat liegt vor, wenn Texte Dritter ganz oder teilweise, wörtlich oder nahezu wörtlich übernommen und als eigene wissenschaftliche Leistung ausgegeben werden. Ein solches Vorgehen widerspricht nicht nur guter wissenschaftlicher Praxis, es ist auch eine Form geistigen Diebstahls und damit eine Verletzung des Urheberrechts. (Resolution des Deutschen Hochschulverbandes vom 17. Juli 2002).

Handelt es sich bei einer Hausarbeit nachweislich um ein Plagiat – z. B. in dem im Internet zugänglich gemachte Hausarbeiten anderer auf die oben beschriebene Art und Weise übernommen wurden –, wird sie als ungenügend bewertet. In diesem Fall wird kein Leistungsnachweis ausgestellt. Auch eine Wiederholung der Arbeit (im Rahmen des entsprechenden Seminars) ist nicht möglich.

Erklärung der / des Studierenden

Hiermit versichere ich, dass ich die vorliegende Arbeit über

....

....

selbstständig verfasst habe, und dass ich keine anderen Quellen und Hilfsmittel als die angegebenen benutzt habe und dass die Stellen der Arbeit, die anderen Werken – auch elektronischen Medien – dem Wortlaut oder Sinn nach entnommen wurden, auf jeden Fall unter Angabe der Quelle als Entlehnung kenntlich gemacht worden sind.

....

Ort, Datum Unterschrift

CPSIA information can be obtained
at www.ICGtesting.com
Printed in the USA
LVHW111352050220
645944LV00001B/128